Understanding Dropouts
Statistics, Strategies, and High-Stakes Testing

Committee on Educational Excellence and Testing Equity

Alexandra Beatty, Ulric Neisser,
William T. Trent, and Jay P. Heubert, *Editors*

Board on Testing and Assessment
Center for Education

Division of Behavioral and Social Sciences and Education

National Research Council

D1264637

NATIONAL ACADEMY PRESS
Washington, D.C.

NATIONAL ACADEMY PRESS   2101 Constitution Avenue, N.W.   **Washington, DC 20418**

NOTICE: The project that is the subject of this report was approved by the Governing Board of the National Research Council, whose members are drawn from the councils of the National Academy of Sciences, the National Academy of Engineering, and the Institute of Medicine. The members of the committee responsible for the report were chosen for their special competences and with regard for appropriate balance.

This study was supported by Contract/Grant No. R305U960001-98A between the National Academy of Sciences and U.S. Department of Education. Any opinions, findings, conclusions, or recommendations expressed in this publication are those of the author(s) and do not necessarily reflect the views of the organizations or agencies that provided support for the project.

International Standard Book Number 0-309-07602-1

Additional copies of this report are available from National Academy Press, 2101 Constitution Avenue, N.W., Lockbox 285, Washington, DC 20055; (800) 624-6242 or (202) 334-3313 (in the Washington metropolitan area); Internet, http://www.nap.edu

Printed in the United States of America

SUGGESTED CITATION: National Research Council (2001) *Understanding Dropouts: Statistics, Strategies, and High-Stakes Testing.* Committee on Educational Excellence and Testing Equity. Alexandra Beatty, Ulric Neisser, William T. Trent, and Jay P. Heubert, Editors. Board on Testing and Assessment, Center for Education, Division of Behavioral and Social Sciences and Education. Washington, DC: National Academy Press.

First Printing, August 2001
Second Printing, November 2001
Third Printing, February 2002
Fourth Printing, October 2002

THE NATIONAL ACADEMIES

National Academy of Sciences
National Academy of Engineering
Institute of Medicine
National Research Council

The **National Academy of Sciences** is a private, nonprofit, self-perpetuating society of distinguished scholars engaged in scientific and engineering research, dedicated to the furtherance of science and technology and to their use for the general welfare. Upon the authority of the charter granted to it by the Congress in 1863, the Academy has a mandate that requires it to advise the federal government on scientific and technical matters. Dr. Bruce M. Alberts is president of the National Academy of Sciences.

The **National Academy of Engineering** was established in 1964, under the charter of the National Academy of Sciences, as a parallel organization of outstanding engineers. It is autonomous in its administration and in the selection of its members, sharing with the National Academy of Sciences the responsibility for advising the federal government. The National Academy of Engineering also sponsors engineering programs aimed at meeting national needs, encourages education and research, and recognizes the superior achievements of engineers. Dr. Wm. A. Wulf is president of the National Academy of Engineering.

The **Institute of Medicine** was established in 1970 by the National Academy of Sciences to secure the services of eminent members of appropriate professions in the examination of policy matters pertaining to the health of the public. The Institute acts under the responsibility given to the National Academy of Sciences by its congressional charter to be an adviser to the federal government and, upon its own initiative, to identify issues of medical care, research, and education. Dr. Kenneth I. Shine is president of the Institute of Medicine.

The **National Research Council** was organized by the National Academy of Sciences in 1916 to associate the broad community of science and technology with the Academy's purposes of furthering knowledge and advising the federal government. Functioning in accordance with general policies determined by the Academy, the Council has become the principal operating agency of both the National Academy of Sciences and the National Academy of Engineering in providing services to the government, the public, and the scientific and engineering communities. The Council is administered jointly by both Academies and the Institute of Medicine. Dr. Bruce M. Alberts and Dr. Wm. A. Wulf are chairman and vice chairman, respectively, of the National Research Council.

COMMITTEE ON EDUCATIONAL EXCELLENCE AND TESTING EQUITY
2000-2001

---

*Did not participate in workshop or deliberations for this report

Contents

Preface

The Committee on Educational Excellence and Testing Equity (CEETE) was formed in 1999 to monitor the effects of standards-based reform on students already at risk for academic failure because of such factors as poverty, lack of proficiency in English, disability, or membership in population subgroups that have been educationally disadvantaged. The committee operates under the aegis of the Board on Testing and Assessment. As a standing committee, CEETE is charged with providing ongoing attention to the specific ways in which educational testing can affect disadvantaged students. CEETE considers focused, topical issues and produces brief syntheses of research, with particular attention to the needs of policy makers at the local, state, and federal levels. By setting both research findings and policy questions in context and, when appropriate, making recommendations, CEETE hopes to serve as a resource for those who must make difficult decisions about students' lives in a fast-paced policy context.

CEETE's first report addressed the challenges of testing English-language learners in ways that are both valid and fair (National Research Council, 2000). In the current report, the committee addresses research and policy questions about students who drop out of school and the role testing may play in their decisions about their schooling. The students about whom the committee is concerned are, for a variety of reasons, more likely than others to drop out of school and have been so for decades. Increasing rates of school completion—and decreasing the gaps in the rates for different groups—are among the goals for education reform, and tests are playing an increasingly significant role in these reform efforts across the country. As more states turn to testing as a means of determining which students will graduate from their systems, the committee was concerned about the potential effects of tests on the rates at which students drop out of school.

A central component of CEETE's charge is to follow up on the 1999 report of the National Research Council's Committee on Appropriate Test Use, *High Stakes: Testing for Tracking, Promotion, and Graduation.* That book offers a number of important findings and recommendations regarding testing, dropouts, and related issues, and this report offers the results of CEETE's further exploration of the issues related to dropouts.

In exploring the available evidence and planning a workshop on the topic, which was held in July 2000, the committee soon found that understanding why students drop out of school, understanding the statistical patterns that characterize school attendance and school leaving—and even obtaining a clear sense of how many students drop out and precisely what it means to drop out of school—were far from straightforward tasks. The committee realized that its task would require not only reviewing available data that might link school completion patterns to exit examination policies, but also setting that discussion in the context of the history of secondary schooling in the United States, exploring the complexities of collecting data about student behavior, and considering research on other aspects of the issue. The report that has resulted from these efforts has three goals: to set current policy discussions in the context of research on dropouts, to offer the committee's synthesis of key research findings, and to offer the committee's recommendations about the ways in which dropout behavior is monitored.

The committee commissioned five papers for presentation at the workshop. This report relies heavily on the work of their authors: John Bishop, Ferran Mane, and Michael Bishop; Sherman Dorn; Mark Dynarski; Phillip Kaufman; Russell Rumberger; and Richard Valencia. Several other experts made valuable contributions as well: Anne Smisko and Robert Meyer made presentations at the workshop, and three scholars with significant relevant expertise, Robert Hauser, David Grissmer, and Aaron Pallas, provided syntheses that were very helpful to the committee's thinking. The committee is indebted to these individuals and to the other workshop participants, who provided a very stimulating exchange of ideas at the workshop.

We also take special note of the efforts of several committee members who took particular responsibility for developing this report—Jay Heubert,

Hank Levin, and John Tobin— and of study director Alix Beatty's work in organizing the workshop and drafting this report. Andrew Tompkins' able assistance with both is gratefully acknowledged as well.

This report has been reviewed in draft form by individuals chosen for their diverse perspectives and technical expertise, in accordance with procedures approved by the Report Review Committee of the National Research Council (NRC). The purpose of this independent review is to provide candid and critical comments that will assist the institution in making the published report as sound as possible and to ensure that the report meets institutional standards for objectivity, evidence, and responsiveness to the study charge. The review comments and draft manuscript remain confidential to protect the integrity of the deliberative process.

We thank the following individuals for their participation in the review of this report: Susan A. Agruso, Charlotte-Mecklenburg School District, North Carolina; Christopher T. Cross, Council for Basic Education; James Karon, Rhode Island Department of Education; Lorraine McDonnell, University of California, Santa Barbara; Bob Rossi, iBuild-Community.com, Los Altos, California; Fritz Scheuren, Urban Institute; Ewart A. C. Thomas, Stanford University.

Although the reviewers listed above have provided many constructive comments and suggestions, they were not asked to endorse the conclusions or recommendations nor did they see the final draft of the report before its release. The review of this report was overseen by John C. Bailar, University of Chicago. Appointed by the National Research Council, he was responsible for making certain that an independent examination of this report was carried out in accordance with institutional procedures and that all review comments were carefully considered. Responsibility for the final content of this report rests entirely with the authoring panel and the institution.

Ulric Neisser and William Trent, Cochairs
Committee on Educational Excellence and Testing Equity

Executive Summary

The role played by testing in the nation's public school system has been increasing steadily—and growing more complicated—for more than 20 years. The Committee on Educational Excellence and Testing Equity (CEETE) was formed to monitor the effects of education reform, particularly testing, on students at risk for academic failure because of poverty, lack of proficiency in English, disability, or membership in population subgroups that have been educationally disadvantaged. The committee recognizes the important potential benefits of standards-based reforms and of test results in revealing the impact of reform efforts on these students. We also recognize the valuable role graduation tests can potentially play in making requirements concrete, in increasing the value of a diploma, and in motivating students and educators alike to work to higher standards. At the same time, we note that educational testing is a complicated endeavor, that reality can fall far short of the model, and that testing cannot by itself provide the desired benefits. If testing is improperly used, it can have negative effects, such as encouraging school leaving, that can hit disadvantaged students hardest. The committee was concerned that the recent proliferation of high school exit examinations could have the unintended effect of increasing dropout rates among students whose rates are already far higher than the average, and has taken a close look at what is known about influences on dropout behavior and at the available data on dropouts and school completion.

CONTEXT

A key to understanding dropout behavior, the factors that may influence it, and also the difficulties facing those who try to measure it, is recognizing that dropping out of school is a process rather than an isolated event. Attributes of schooling, individual personality traits, home environment, and the economic context in which students live all influence their progress through school. Isolating a single cause for this process is thus nearly impossible. However, the factors most associated with dropping out suggest strategies to encourage students at risk to stay in school.

Research supports common sense in showing that dropping out is a major life event to which a host of influences contribute in the course of a young person's life. The significance of dropping out has also shifted over time. During the nineteenth century and the early decades of the twentieth century, a young person who failed to complete 12 years of schooling by the age of 18 or 19 was hardly unusual, and the existence of many such young people was not identified as a social problem. Since roughly the middle of the twentieth century, however, teenagers have been expected to stay in school until graduation, and the employment prospects for those who do not have dimmed.

At the same time, avenues for young people have proliferated. Students who opt out or are pushed out (by school discipline policies or other school actions) of traditional high schools can attend alternative programs or take the General Educational Development (GED) Test instead of graduating—although these alternatives are often not equivalent to a standard high-school diploma in terms of a student's future opportunities for education and employment. Students drop in or out of school or may return to school or take the GED years after their expected graduation dates. Moreover, in a society characterized by both high rates of immigration and high rates of internal mobility, students frequently move among schools, districts, and states.

DATA NEEDS

Those circumstances make it particularly difficult for both researchers and school systems to define and count dropouts. As a consequence, a variety of means for doing so have been devised for different purposes. Results, even for the same jurisdiction, can seem to be in conflict when different means of counting are used, and observers can be left either misinformed or confused about the scope and nature of the problem. Researchers have developed a number of definitions of dropouts and a number of ways of collecting information about them. These definitions and methods are not widely understood. Debates about the effects of testing and other reforms have been significantly complicated by the lack of clarity in dropout statistics. Moreover, data on several important aspects of school completion are not currently collected. The committee has considered this situation and offers five recommendations regarding data collection. The committee recognizes that the burden of data collection for states and districts is already considerable, but we conclude that there is no substitute for reliable information about these important issues.

While the consequences of dropping out of school have been well established, as have the ways in which earning a GED credential in lieu of a traditional diploma may affect later outcomes, the nature and implications of other alternatives to graduation have not. In view of the significant numbers of students who currently pursue these alternatives, it is important to understand what these alternatives involve.

Recommendation 1: The committee recommends to states and districts and to both researchers and funders of research that priority be placed on collecting key data that are disaggregated to allow monitoring of such populations as different minority groups, English-language learners, and students with disabilities. These data should cover:

- which students, and how many students, are receiving credentials, including GED certification, that are different from the generally prevailing standards for high-school graduation;
- the nature of the academic requirements that lead to such credentials, and the extent to which those requirements are different from the generally prevailing standards for high school graduation;
- the processes by which students are directed to or choose to pursue such alternate credentials; and
- the later educational and employment outcomes for the students who receive these credentials.

Studies show that although GED certification can be beneficial for many students, it has less value than a standard diploma as a tool for pursuing both education and employment. It is important that policy makers, educators, parents, and students be aware of the distinctions among available credentials.

Recommendation 2: The committee recommends that officials at the school, district, and state levels disaggregate the data they already collect on school completers by the type of certificate awarded, including those awarded for passing the GED, and should make clear what knowledge and skills are represented by each credential. States, schools, and districts should also distinguish between GED holders and high school graduates in reporting data on school completion. These data should be disaggregated to allow monitoring of such populations as different minority groups, English-language learners, and students with disabilities.

The committee concludes that current means of collecting district-, state-, and national-level data on students' progress through school and into the workforce, while valuable, are insufficient to inform policy makers and the public.

Recommendation 3: The committee recommends that policy makers, researchers, and funders of research consider the urgent need for the following kinds of additional data (disaggregated to allow monitoring of such populations as different minority groups, English-language learners, and students with disabilities):

• data that allow valid comparisons across states and, possibly, across smaller jurisdictions;
• longitudinal data that allow tracking of a greater diversity of student pathways, such as participation in alternatives to traditional secondary schooling and the earning of alternatives to the traditional diploma;
• data that allow separate reporting on the progress of students who take the GED or follow other alternate pathways, both while they are in school and after they leave school, whether they are employed, unemployed, or participating in postsecondary education;
• data that allow improved tracking of students at risk for dropping out because of factors that may be apparent in elementary and middle school, such as temporary dropping out in early grades, absenteeism, retention in grade, and the like. Such data could assist jurisdictions in identifying populations of students in need of intervention and in evaluating the success of their efforts to intervene. Such data could also be used to improve public understanding of school completion and the demands on school systems.

Part of the difficulty with currently available data is that they are collected by a variety of entities for a variety of purposes at the state, district, and school levels, as well as at the federal level. The adoption of a single measure that would allow comparisons across jurisdictions would address some of the difficulties in the current policy discussion, but it would have negative consequences as well. The various measures exist because of the complexities of what needs to be measured, and each provides valuable information. CEETE concludes that more, not less, information about dropout behavior is needed, but believes that greater clarity and coordination is needed as well.

Recommendation 4: The committee recommends that the U.S. Department of Education provide leadership and oversight in efforts to coordinate data collection and establish long-term objectives for collecting what is needed. Data available from the U.S. Department of Labor should be considered as part of this effort.

In considering the need for additional data about school completion, it is important to note one population of students who have not traditionally been classed among dropouts: students who complete the requirements for twelfth grade but are unable to pass a test that is required for a diploma. More detailed information about how many students are in this category in each of the states that rely on exit examinations is needed. Improved understanding of the possible differences between these students and students who drop out of school before the end of twelfth grade, and about the effects of failing the exam on these students' future education and employment will be an important part of understanding the effects of exit exams.

Recommendation 5: The committee recommends that jurisdictions that administer exit exams collect detailed data on students who complete the twelfth grade but fail exit exams and so do not graduate (disaggregated to allow monitoring of such populations as different minority groups, English-language learners, and students with disabilities).

FACTORS ASSOCIATED WITH DROPPING OUT

Though proof of causation is elusive, much is known about the factors most closely associated with dropping out:

- A number of school-related factors, such as high concentrations of low-achieving students and less-qualified teachers, for example, are associated with higher dropout rates. Other factors, such as small school settings and individualized attention to students, are associated with lower dropout rates.
- Many aspects of home life and socioeconomic status are associated with dropout behavior.
- Typically, contributing factors interact in a gradual process of disengagement from school over many years.

Ongoing patterns of absenteeism, poor grades, and poor achievement on tests even early in elementary school are linked to dropping out later on. Retention in grade is clearly associated with subsequent decisions to drop out of school. Other characteristics of schooling, such as the composition of the school and its climate, practices, and resources may affect dropout behavior as well. Many of these factors suggest that dropout prevention programs targeted at high school or even middle school students hold less promise for helping students than do earlier interventions. Thus, early intervention for students who show signs of academic difficulty or disengagement from school is very important.

A number of factors outside of school have also been associated with an increased likelihood of dropping out, and the evidence suggests that these factors can interact to increase the risk. Hispanic students are the most likely to drop out, and African American students are more likely to than whites. Students whose families' incomes are in the lowest 20 percent of the population are far more likely to drop out than are nonpoor students. An increased risk of academic difficulty and dropping out is also evident for students who live in single-parent families, those from large families, and those who become parents themselves.

Conclusion: The committee concludes that identifying students with risk factors early in their careers (preschool through elementary school) and providing them with ongoing support, remediation, and counseling are likely to be the most promising means of encouraging them to stay in school. Using individual risk factors to identify likely dropouts with whom to intervene, particularly among students at the ninth-grade level and beyond, is difficult. Evidence about interventions done at this stage suggests that their effectiveness is limited.

THE ROLE OF TESTING

Distinctions among different kinds of tests are key to understanding the effects they may have on students. The effects of more rigorous, content-based tests may be very different from the effects of basic-skills tests. The way in which testing programs are aligned with curricular requirements and standards, as well as other aspects of the educational system, are also central for understanding their role and effects. To be truly informative, evaluations of the impact of exit tests should clearly distinguish among different kinds of tests and those used for different purposes.

At this early stage in the progress of many state reforms there is insufficient evidence to determine conclusively what effect, if any, exit examinations have on dropout rates. Indeed, the likelihood is that the effects of these tests will vary significantly, depending on how they are constructed and implemented and on how their results are used. However, there is reason to believe that high-stakes testing at any level may sometimes be used in ways that have unintended harmful effects on students at particular risk for academic failure because of poverty, lack of proficiency in English, disability, and membership in population subgroups that have been educationally disadvantaged. Although the precise relationship between graduation testing and dropping out of school is still in dispute, it is clear that retention in grade is a very strong predictor of dropping out.

Conclusion: Given the difficulty and cost of preventing students from dropping out once the process of disengagement from school has begun, it is clear that neither requiring a student to retake the grade nor promoting a failing student is, by itself, a sufficient response to his or her academic difficulty. The value and importance of addressing struggling students' difficulties directly and specifically as soon as they are apparent are paramount. Moreover, the strong association between retention in grade and dropping out suggests that retention is usually not a beneficial intervention.

1

Background and Context

Failure to complete high school has been recognized as a social problem in the United States for decades and, as discussed below, the individual and social costs of dropping out are considerable. Social scientists, policy makers, journalists, and the public have pondered questions about why students drop out, how many drop out, what happens to dropouts, and how young people might be kept from dropping out. Currently, many voices are arguing about the effects of standards-based reforms and graduation tests on students' decisions to drop out and about which dropout counts are correct. A significant body of research has examined questions about dropouts, and this section of the report provides an overview of current knowledge about these young people. We begin with a look at the history of school completion.

CHANGING EXPECTATIONS FOR STUDENTS

Expectations for the schooling of adolescents in the United States have changed markedly in the past 100 years. Indeed, the very notion of adolescence as a phase of life distinct from both childhood and adulthood came into common parlance only in the first decades of the twentieth century, at roughly the same time that educators began to develop increasingly ambitious goals for the schooling of students beyond the eighth grade (*Education Week*, 2000:36). At the turn of the last century, as Sherman Dorn noted in the paper he prepared for the workshop, "fewer than one of every ten adolescents graduated from high school. Today, roughly three of every four teens can expect to earn a diploma through a regular high school program" (Dorn, 2000:4).

High school in the early part of the century was a growing phenomenon, but it was still made available primarily to middle- and upper-class students and was generally focused on rigorous college preparatory work. At the turn of the century, the lack of a high school diploma did not necessarily deter young people from going on to successful careers in business or politics. As the number of students enrolled in high school grew, from approximately 500,000 in 1900 to 2.4 million in 1920 and then to 6.5 million in 1940, notions of the purpose of postelementary schooling were evolving.

Dorn provided the committee with an overview of trends in graduation rates over the twentieth century, noting three features of the overall trend that stand out:[1] (1) a steady increase in graduation rates throughout the first half of the twentieth century; (2) a decrease around the years during and immediately after the Second World War; (3) a plateau beginning with the cohort of students born during the 1950s. He discussed possible explanations for these changes in school completion rates.

One possible explanation is the influence of changes in the labor market. A number of developments had the effect of excluding increasing numbers of young people from full-time employment in the early decades of the twentieth century, including the mechanization of agriculture, increases in immigration, and the passage of new child labor laws. As teenagers had more difficulty finding work, increasing numbers of them stayed enrolled in school. The dip during the later 1940s is correspondingly explained by the fact that it was not only adult women who moved into the workforce to replace male workers who left employment for military service, but also teenagers of both sexes. The postwar dip and plateau also correlates with the growing availability of part-time employment and other labor opportunities for teenagers, which challenged the perception that completing school was important to financial success.

Dorn describes a pattern in which participation in successive levels of schooling gradually increases until the pressure spills over into the next level. Increasing proportions of the potential student population tend to

---

[1]Dorn based his discussion of the trendlines on the Current Population Survey, census data, and state and district administrative data sources.

participate in schooling to a given level until saturation is reached—that is, until virtually all are enrolled. Expectations regarding participation in the next level then expand, and the pattern is repeated. In the United States, the norm has moved from primary schooling, to the eighth-grade level, and then to high school completion. State laws regarding school enrollment have moved along with these expectations. Currently, most states require that students stay enrolled through the age of 16. The steady increase in high school enrollment during the first half of the century thus reflects the gradual development of the now widely shared conviction that all teenagers should complete high school. Current political discourse reflects a developing expectation that the majority of students will not just complete high school but also participate in some form of higher education.

It was not until the 1960s that dropping out was widely considered a social problem because it was not until midcentury that sufficient percentages of young people were graduating from high school so that those who did not could be viewed as deviating from the norm. Dorn illustrated the views of dropping out that were becoming current in that period with this 1965 quotation from sociologist Lucius Cervantes (quoted in Dorn, 2000:19):

> It is from this hard core of dropouts that a high proportion of the gangsters, hoodlums, drug-addicted, government-dependent prone, irresponsible and illegitimate parents of tomorrow will be predictably recruited.

A number of scholars have argued that as enrollments have increased, high schools' missions have evolved. Many jurisdictions responded to the arrival of waves of immigrants by making it more difficult for families to avoid enrolling their children in school, arguing that public schools were the best vehicle for assimilating these new citizens and would-be citizens (*Education Week*, 2000:4). As the children of the lower and middle classes entered high school, however, expectations and graduation standards were lowered. Thus, the postwar plateau might also be explained by the notion that, as Dorn put it, "by the 1960s high schools really had succeeded at becoming the prime custodians for adolescents" (Dorn, 2000:10). If high schools were actually providing little benefit for the students on the lower rungs of the socioeconomic ladder, according to this reasoning, there was little motivation for increasing the graduation rate from 70 or 80 percent to 100 percent.

Another notable trend was the general decrease in gaps between completion rates for whites and nonwhites and other population subgroups.

Observers have noted that this narrowing of the gap relates to the saturation effect described earlier—completion rates for Hispanics and African Americans have moved up while those for whites have remained level (Cameron and Heckman, 1993a:5). At the same time, however, alternative notions of school completion have proliferated (discussed in greater detail below). Dorn called attention to the fact that in Florida six different types of diplomas are available and that other states have adopted similar means of marking differing levels of achievement. The categories of school completion are not fixed and apparently not of equivalent value; it may be that many minority students who have converted statistically from dropouts to school completers have in fact moved to an in-between status that needs to be better understood. This circumstance significantly complicates the task of statisticians and others who attempt to keep track of students' progress through school. It also complicates policy discussions about social goals for young people, expectations of the education system, and possible solutions to the problem of dropouts.

LOOKING AT DROPOUTS

A recent report from the National Center for Education Statistics (NCES) shows that five percent of all young adults who were enrolled in grades 10-12 (519,000 of 10,464,000) dropped out of school between October 1998 and October 1999 (National Center for Education Statistics, 2000:iii). That report provides a wealth of other important information, noting, for example, that Hispanic and African American students are significantly more likely than white students to drop out and that students from poor families are far more likely to drop out than are students from nonpoor families. The report provides information on trends in dropout rates over time and comparisons among students by age, racial and ethnic characteristics, and the like.

The statistical information in this and other reports is valuable, but it provides only a snapshot of the situation across the country. General statistical reports are not designed to reveal the effects of particular policies, programs, and educational approaches on particular groups of students, but variations in the numbers suggest possible sources of more detailed understanding. School completion rates reported by states and districts show wide variation, for example, from 74.5 percent for Nevada to 92.9 percent for Maine. The rates at which students complete school vary over time and are different for different population subgroups, regions, and kinds of schools, and for students who differ in other ways. (The school completion rate is only one of several ways of measuring dropout behavior; see discussion below). The reported data (from NCES) suggest that particular factors are associated with dropping out, such as single-parent homes, teenage pregnancy, history of academic difficulty, and retention in grade. Other researchers have identified specific school factors that are associated with dropping out, discussed below.

The rates can be calculated in different ways, which means that dropout or school completion rates for the same jurisdiction can look very different, depending on which method is used. Indeed, there is no single dropout measure that can be relied on for analysis; there are many rates based on different definitions and measures, collected by different agents for different purposes. The NCES report, for example, opens by presenting two calculations of dropouts, 5 percent and 11 percent, respectively, for slightly different groups, as well as a percentage of school completers, 85.9 percent (2000:iii).

The confusion about counting dropouts is not surprising when one considers the challenges of counting students in different categories. Numerous decisions can drastically affect the count: At what point in the school year should student enrollment be counted? Should it be done at every grade? How long should a student's absence from school be to count as dropping out? What age ranges should be considered? What about private and charter schools and students who are home-schooled? In most school districts and states, significant numbers of students move into and out of their jurisdictions each year, so school careers are difficult to track. Even within a jurisdiction, many students follow irregular pathways that are also difficult to track—they may drop out of school temporarily, perhaps more than once, before either completing or leaving for good. Different jurisdictions face different statistical challenges, depending on the composition of their student populations. Districts with high immigrant populations may have large numbers of young people who arrive with little documentation of their previous schooling, so that determining which among them have completed school is difficult. What students do after dropping out is also highly variable. Alternative educational and vocational programs, which may or may not be accredited means of completing secondary schooling requirements, have proliferated. A significant number of students take the General Educational Development (GED) Test every year; many (but not all) of them receive school completion credentials from their states.

Tracking dropout behavior is clearly messy. In response, statisticians have devised a variety of ways of measuring the behavior: status dropout rates, event dropout rates, school completion rates, and more. Unfortunately, the many measures often lead to confusion or misunderstanding among people trying to use or understand the data. A later section of this report addresses in greater detail some of the reasons why measuring this aspect of student behavior is complicated and describe what is meant by some of the different measures that are available. First, however, it is worth summarizing the general picture of high school dropouts that has emerged from accumulated research. These general observations describe trends that are evident regardless of the method by which dropouts are counted.

WHO DROPS OUT

The overall rate at which students drop out of school has declined gradually in recent decades, but is currently stable. A number of student characteristics have been consistently correlated with dropping out over the past few decades.[2] First and most important, dropping out is significantly more prevalent among Hispanic and African American students, among students in poverty, among students in urban schools, among English-language learners, and among students with disabilities than among those who do not have these characteristics. The characteristics of the students most likely to drop out illustrate one of the keys to understanding the phenomenon: that dropping out is a process that may begin in the early years of elementary school, not an isolated event that occurs during the last few years of high school. The process has been described as one of gradual disengagement from school. The particular stages and influences vary widely, but the discernible pattern is an interaction among characteristics of the family and home environment and characteristics of a student's experience in school.

Family and Home Characteristics

Income In general, students at low income levels are more likely to drop out of school than are those at higher levels. NCES reports that in

---

[2]Data in this section are taken from National Center for Education Statistics (1996, 2000), which are based on the Current Population Survey. The numbers are event dropout rates.

1999 the dropout rate for students whose families were in the lowest 20 percent of income distribution was 11 percent; for students whose families fall in the middle 60 percent it was 5 percent; and for students from families in the top 20 percent it was 2 percent.

Race/Ethnicity Both Hispanic and African American students are more likely to drop out than are white students, with the rate for Hispanic students being consistently the highest. In 1999, 28.6 percent of Hispanic students dropped out of school, compared with 12.6 percent of black students and 7.3 percent of white students. It is important to note that among Hispanic youths, the dropout rate is significantly higher for those who were not born in the United States (44.2%) than for those who were (16.1%). Two important issues relate to this last point: first, a significant number of foreign-born Hispanic young people have never been enrolled in a U.S. school. Second, the majority of those who were never enrolled have been reported as speaking English "not well" or "not at all." The status of Hispanic young people offers an illustration of the complexities of counting dropouts. Young people who have never been enrolled in a U.S. school but have no diploma typically show up in measures of status dropout rates (people of a certain age who have no diploma) but not in measures of event dropout rates (students enrolled in one grade but not the next who have not received a diploma or been otherwise accounted for). This issue is addressed in greater detail below.

Family Structure Research has shown an increased risk of academic difficulty or dropping out for students who live in single-parent families, those from large families, and those, especially girls, who have become parents themselves. Other factors have been noted as well, such as having parents who have completed fewer years of schooling or who report providing little support for their children's education, such as providing a specific place to study and reading materials.

School-Related Characteristics

History of Poor Academic Performance Not surprisingly, poor grades and test scores are associated with an increased likeliness to drop out, as is enrollment in remedial courses.

Educational Engagement Researchers have used several measures of students' educational engagement, including hours of television watched, hours spent on homework, hours spent at paid employment, and frequency of attending class without books and other necessary materials. Each of these factors has been associated with increased likeliness to encounter academic difficulties and to drop out. That is, the more time a student spends at a job or watching television, the more likely he or she is to drop out. Students who spend relatively little time on homework and who are more likely to attend school unprepared are similarly at increased risk of dropping out.

Academic Delay Students who are older than the normal range for the grade in which they are enrolled are significantly more likely to drop out of school than are those who are not. Similarly, students who have received fewer than the required number of academic credits for their grade are more likely to drop out than other students are.

Interactions

Risk factors tend to cluster together and to have cumulative effects. The children of families in poverty, for example, have a greater risk of academic difficulty than do other children, and they are also at greater risk for poor health, early and unwanted pregnancies, and criminal behavior, each of which is associated with an increased risk of dropping out (National Center for Education Statistics, 1996:11). Urban schools and districts consistently report the highest dropout rates; the annual rate for all urban districts currently averages 10 percent, and in many urban districts it is much higher (Balfanz and Legters, 2001:22). Student populations in these districts are affected by the risk factors associated with dropping out, particularly poverty, in greater numbers than are students in other districts.

WHY STUDENTS DROP OUT

Students who have dropped out of school have given three common reasons (*ERIC Digest*, 1987:1):

- A dislike of school and a view that school is boring and not relevant to their needs;
  - Low academic achievement, poor grades, or academic failure; and
  - A need for money and a desire to work full-time.

These responses in no way contradict the statistical portrait of students who drop out in the United States, but they offer a somewhat different perspective from which to consider the many factors that influence students' decisions about school and work. Shifts in the labor market can have profound effects on students' behavior that are evident in national statistics, particularly those that track changes over many years. Scholars have also identified socioeconomic factors that correlate with the likelihood of a student's dropping out. However, each student whose life is captured in dropout statistics is an individual reacting to a unique set of circumstances. The circumstances that cause a particular student to separate from school before completing the requirements for a diploma can rarely be summed up easily, and rarely involve only one factor. Nevertheless, educators and policy makers alike see that dropping out of school diminishes young people's life chances in significant ways, and look for ways to understand both why they do it and how they might be prevented from doing it.

Dropping Out as a Process

Rumberger summarizes a key message from the research on the factors associated with dropping out:

> Although dropping out is generally considered a status or educational outcome that can readily be measured at a particular point in time, it is more appropriately viewed as a process of disengagement that occurs over time. And warning signs for students at risk of dropping out often appear in elementary school, providing ample time to intervene (Rumberger, 2000:25).

Beginning with some points that can be difficult to discern in the complex statistics about dropping out, Rumberger noted that the percentage of young people who complete high school through an alternative to the traditional course requirements and diploma (through the GED or a vocational or other alternative) has grown: 4 percent used an alternative means in 1988 while 10 percent did so in 1998—though the calculated school completion rate among 18- to 24-year-olds remained constant at about 85 percent (Rumberger, 2000:7). Several longitudinal studies show that a much larger percentage of students than are captured in event or status dropout calculations drop out of school temporarily for one or more periods during high school. Doing so is associated with later dropping out for good, with a decreased likelihood of enrolling in postsecondary schooling, and with an increased likelihood of unemployment.

Focusing on the process that leads to the ultimate decision to drop out, Rumberger stresses the importance of interaction among a variety of contributing factors: "if many factors contribute to this phenomenon over a long period of time, it is virtually impossible to demonstrate a causal connection between any single factor and the decision to quit school" (Rumberger, 2001:4). Instead, researchers have looked for ways to organize the factors that seem to be predictive of dropping out in ways that can be useful in efforts to intervene and prevent that outcome. As noted above, two basic categories are characteristics of students, their families and their home circumstances, and characteristics of their schooling.

Rumberger pays particular attention to the concept of engagement with school. Absenteeism and discipline problems are strong predictors of dropping out, even for students not experiencing academic difficulties. More subtle indicators of disengagement from school, such as moving from school to school, negative attitude toward school, and minor discipline problems can show up as early as elementary and middle school as predictors of a subsequent decision to drop out. The role of retention in grade is very important in this context:

> . . . students who were retained in grades 1 to 8 were four times more likely to drop out between grades 8 and 10 than students who were not retained, even after controlling for socioeconomic status, 8th grade school performance, and a host of background and school factors (Rumberger, 2000:15).

Rumberger's work confirms other research on family characteristics that are associated with dropping out, particularly the finding that belonging to families lower in socioeconomic status and those headed by a single parent are both risk factors for students. He also looked at research on the role that less concrete factors may play. Stronger relationships between parents and children seem to reduce the risk of dropping out, as does being the child of parents who "monitor and regulate [the child's] activities, provide emotional support, encourage decision-making . . . and are generally more involved in [the child's] schooling" (Rumberger, 2000:17).

At the workshop, David Grissmer touched on some other factors that don't make their way into national statistics but that could play a significant role for many young people. He pointed to studies of hyperactivity and attention-deficit disorder that indicate that while the percentage of all young people affected is small, roughly 5 percent, the percentage of high school dropouts affected is much larger—perhaps as much as 40 percent. He noted that dyslexia, depression, and other cognitive or mental health problems can have significant effects on students' capacity to learn and flourish in the school environment, but that these situations are often overlooked in statistical analyses.

Schools also play a role in outcomes for students. Rumberger presented data showing that when results are controlled for students' background characteristics, dropout rates for schools still vary widely. Rumberger's (2000) review of the literature on school effects identifies several key findings:

- The social composition of the student body seems to influence student achievement—and affect the dropout rate. That is, students who attend schools with high concentrations of students with characteristics that increase their likelihood of dropping out, but who don't have those characteristics themselves, are nevertheless more likely to drop out. This finding relates to the fact that dropout rates are consistently significantly higher for urban schools and districts than for others (Balfanz and Legters, 2001:1).
- Some studies suggest that school resources can influence the dropout rate through the student-teacher ratio and possibly through teacher quality.
- The climate, policies, and practices of a school may have effects on dropping out. Indicators of the school climate, such as attendance rates and numbers of students enrolled in advanced courses, may be predictive of dropping out. There is some evidence that other factors, such as school size, structure, and governance, may also have effects.

Interventions

A variety of different kinds of evidence point to the importance of early attention to the problems that are associated with subsequent dropping out. The correspondence between the many risk factors that have been enumerated is not, however, either linear or foolproof. Dynarski (2000) notes that despite strong associations between a variety of characteristics and dropping out, using individual risk factors as predictors is tricky: research that has evaluated the predictive value of risk factors has shown that the one "that was best able to predict whether middle school students were dropouts—high absenteeism—correctly identified dropouts only 16 percent of the time" (Dynarski, 2000:9).

A quantitative look at the effectiveness of dropout prevention programs can seem sobering, but it is important to bear in mind that even a perfectly successful program—one that kept every potential dropout in school—would affect only a small fraction of students. Any program that is an attempt to intervene in time to prevent dropping out must begin with a group of students who share defined risk factors, but of whom only a fraction would actually have dropped out. That is, even among groups of students with many risk factors, the dropout rate rarely goes over approximately 15 percent, and it is only these 15 of 100 students who receive an intervention whose fates could potentially be changed. When resources are limited, correctly identifying the students who will benefit most from intervention (those who are most likely to drop out) is clearly important. However, since many different kinds of factors affect dropout behavior, using them as predictors is not easy. This point is also relevant to Rumberger's point that if numerous factors contribute to a multiyear process of dropping out, isolating a cause or an effective predictor would logically be very difficult.

Though the quantitative evidence of effectiveness is not overwhelming, Dynarski (2000) used the results of a Department of Education study of the effectiveness of dropout prevention programs to provide a description of some of the strategies that seem to work best. Providing individual-level counseling to students emerged as a key tool for changing students' thinking about their education. Another tool was creating smaller school settings, even within a large school, if necessary. Students are more likely to become alienated and disengaged from school in larger settings, and are likely to receive less individualized attention from teachers and staff.[3] Not surprisingly, providing counseling and creating smaller school settings requires more staff, and, in turn, the expenditure of more resources per pupil (Dynarski, 2000).

Others who have explored the effectiveness of dropout prevention programs have come to conclusions that amplify and support Dynarski's findings. McPartland and Jordan (2001) advocate, among other things, that high schools be restructured to provide smaller school settings and to both increase student engagement with school and strengthen students' relationships with school staff. McPartland has also suggested specific supports for students who enter high school unprepared for challenging academic work,

---

[3]The work of Lee and Burkam (2001), Fine (1987), and others on the structure of high schools is relevant to this point.

including extra time to complete courses and remediation outside of school hours.

In summary, the committee finds several important messages in the research on dropout behavior:

- A number of school-related factors, such as high concentrations of low-achieving students, and less-qualified teachers, for example, are associated with higher dropout rates. Other factors, such as small school settings and individualized attention, are associated with lower dropout rates.
- Many aspects of home life and socioeconomic status are associated with dropout behavior.
- Typically, contributing factors interact in a gradual process of disengagement from school over many years.

Conclusion: The committee concludes that identifying students with risk factors early in their careers (preschool through elementary school) and providing them with ongoing support, remediation, and counseling are likely to be the most promising means of encouraging them to stay in school. Using individual risk factors to identify likely dropouts with whom to intervene, particularly among students at the ninth-grade level and beyond, is difficult. Evidence about interventions done at this stage suggests that their effectiveness is limited.

2

What Completion Means and Why It's Important

I t would seem to be an easy matter to determine whether or not a student has completed secondary school, but doing so is complicated by a growing number of alternatives to the traditional path of completing four years of coursework in an accredited secondary school and receiving a diploma. As Americans have developed the expectation that all students ought to complete high school and receive a credential, jurisdictions have responded by developing a wider variety of pathways for the students they serve. Sherman Dorn took note of the growing trend (beginning as early as the 1920s) for the mission of many high schools to be viewed as providing primarily vocational training and other programs for students not believed capable of challenging academic work. State- and local-level officials sought ways to provide diplomas for all without compromising the education they were offering to college-bound and other academically oriented students. Some cities established selective public high schools, such as Central High School in Philadelphia and Bronx High School of Science in New York City, that drew students from across the district who wished to pursue ambitious programs and were able to pass entrance requirements. Others established vocational schools for nonacademic students.

Tracking within schools is another method by which students have been placed on different trajectories; more recently, many districts have developed tiered diploma systems that often mirror the academic tracks. Currently, across all 50 states, 15 different types of diplomas are available, and only 8 states (Arizona, Idaho, Minnesota, New Jersey, Oklahoma,

Rhode Island, South Dakota, and Washington) offer just one kind (Dorn, 2000:16). In 12 states an honors diploma is available, while 35 states offer some combination of individual education plan (IEP) diplomas (for students with some kind of disability) and certificates of attendance. For students who are being educated at home, states have different means of addressing the need for certification. The precise nature of what students must do to earn these different kinds of diplomas and the degree of variety they represent have not been well documented.

Alternative programs and certificates have been developed in response to the reality that secondary students' needs, goals, strengths, and weaknesses differ, and we recognize that these alternatives can offer valuable options for many students. However, the alternatives and their effects on students' lives need to be better understood. Meanwhile, researchers have already looked closely at outcomes for students who obtain a high school diploma, those who do not, and those who obtain General Educational Development (GED) certification. There are clear differences in the outcomes for these three groups which indicate that obtaining a diploma has concrete benefits for young people the effects of which can last throughout their lives.

THE GED

Currently, more than 800,000 people take a GED Test every year, hoping to obtain a certificate that will be equivalent to a high school diploma in the eyes of employers and postsecondary institutions. However, the consequences of GED certification are not the same as those of earning a traditional high school diploma. The lifetime earnings of GED recipients are significantly lower than those of high school graduates, and they are not substantially higher than those of dropouts (see below). Moreover, while those who take the GED demonstrate some skills and knowledge by doing so, they have, presumably, missed something of value by dropping out of school.[1]

The GED is described by the American Council on Education (ACE), which develops and administers it through the GED Testing Service, as a measure of the "academic skills and knowledge expected of high school

---

[1]Not all people who take the GED are dropouts. Many immigrants, for example, whose school completion credentials are not recognized in the United States, need GED certification to pursue further education or employment.

graduates in the U.S. or Canada." The GED was originally developed for veterans who had left high school to serve in World War II. It was not, however, widely considered a solution to the dropout problem until decades later. Today, according to the ACE, "about one in seven high school diplomas issued in the United States each year is based on passing the GED Tests" (American Council on Education, 2001).

The GED is a battery of five tests made up of multiple-choice questions and an essay. The five tested areas are writing, social studies, science, interpreting literature and the arts, and mathematics. The questions are also categorized according to Bloom's taxonomy of educational objectives: comprehension, application, analysis, synthesis, and evaluation. The scale on which the GED tests are scored is based on the performance of graduating high school seniors, and the test is intended to provide an opportunity for nongraduates to demonstrate that they can match or exceed the performance of a defined set of graduating students. Individual states set passing scores, which vary significantly.

According to the GED Testing Service website (American Council on Education, 2001), "More than 95 percent of employers in the U.S. consider GED graduates the same as traditional high school graduates in regard to hiring, salary, and opportunity for advancement." The percentage of students who receive the GED instead of a traditional diploma has grown from 2 percent in 1954 to 14 percent in 1987 (Cameron and Heckman, 1993:4). A number of scholars have considered the consequences for students of obtaining a GED diploma in lieu of a traditional one and have reached somewhat more complicated assessments. Richard Murnane and others have found that while those who have earned a GED diploma have greater earnings than those who drop out of school, "Acquisition of the GED credential is not a powerful strategy for escaping poverty" (Murnane et al., 1995:144). These scholars concluded that the primary benefit of earning the GED might lie in the fact that participating in the process leads young people to job-training programs and entry-level jobs. Additional research by Murnane et al. (1999) has found that the benefits of acquiring the GED may not apply equally to all students—that those who have higher skills at the point of dropping out fare better than those with lower ones, even if both earn a GED.

Cameron and Heckman found significant differences in the outcomes for GED recipients and traditional graduates. The found that "dropouts and [holders of the GED] have comparably poor wages, earnings, hours of work, unemployment experiences, and job tenure" (Cameron and Heckman, 1993:43). They note also that the rise in GED certification, which has been particularly sharp for Hispanics and African Americans, accounts for a significant portion of the narrowing of the gap that has been observed between dropout rates for these two groups and whites. Cameron and Heckman observe that the growth of many federal and state adult education programs that support or encourage GED certification may have had the paradoxical effect of encouraging some young people to move away from traditional schooling (Cameron and Heckman, 1993a:36-43).

Murnane et al. (1999:13) found differences in patterns of postsecondary enrollment among conventional high school graduates, GED holders, and so-called "permanent" dropouts. By their analysis of data from the High School and Beyond Survey of the National Center for Education Statistics, many more GED recipients (30%) than dropouts (8%) obtain some postsecondary credit. However, while 36 percent of graduates complete four or more years of postsecondary education, less than 2 percent of GED holders do so.

Others have noted that while perceptions of the purpose of the GED have shifted, the benefits are not equal for all test takers (Chaplin, 1999). While it is clear that obtaining the GED is preferable to not receiving any credential, the benefits seem to be greatest for adults who have already moved well past high school age and for minorities. The GED Testing Service originally had a policy of recommending that GED test takers be age 20 or older because the test was not designed as an alternative to high school. The age has since been reduced to 16. Noting that currently more than 50,000 16- and 17-year-olds earn GED certification each year and that the percentage of 16- to 19-year-olds whose credential is GED certification in lieu of a diploma has been increasing, Chaplin (1999) has argued that allowing teenagers to take the exam may have the unintended effect of encouraging some of them to drop out of school. It is also worth noting that the military no longer treats GED certification as equivalent to a diploma in evaluating recruits. While the GED clearly offers a material benefit for many young people who leave high school and wish to continue their education or improve their job prospects, statistically, GED holders are more similar to dropouts than to school completers in terms of their educational and employment outcomes.

TABLE 2-1   Impact of Schooling on the Annual Earnings
and Unemployment Rates of Males

Schooling	Earnings (1992 $)	Unemployment Rate— 1992
BA or more	$38,115	4.8 %
Assoc. Degree	$31,855	5.5 %
13-15 Yrs	$27,279	7.4 %
12 Yrs	$22,494	8.2 %
9-11 Yrs	$16,194	12.4 %

SOURCE: Bishop et al., 2000:4.

ECONOMIC CONSEQUENCES OF DROPPING OUT

The alternative of withdrawing from any kind of schooling before receiving a diploma is still the path taken by a significant number of young people. Researchers have found a number of ways to explore the consequences of this decision. The economic consequences are significant: The earnings of those who have not finished high school are lower than the earnings of those who have graduated throughout their working lives. A further gap exists between the earnings of those who have finished high school and those with further education, as illustrated in Table 2-1, which also shows the association between schooling and the unemployment rate.

For most students who fail to complete school, that outcome reflects many years of academic difficulty or missed opportunities to learn. While some high school dropouts go on to obtain further education, the majority do not. Comparisons of student performance on standardized tests show, not surprisingly, that staying in school increases achievement gains in all subjects (Ekstrom et al., 1987:56). Some research has suggested an association between dropping out and the likelihood of subsequent criminal activity. Pettit and Western (2001) found, for example, that the risk of being incarcerated by age 30-34 is significantly higher for young men (particularly young black men) who have not completed high school than for those who have.[2] Although statistical relationships between dropping out of

---

[2]The racial differences found by Pettit and Western are striking. For example, among males born in 1955-1959, 21.9 percent of the blacks who had not completed high school were incarcerated by 1989, compared with 3.1 percent of white male noncompleters.

school and other negative outcomes, such as incarceration, are suggestive, they do not establish causation. It may be that other factors associated with both dropping out and incarceration account for some portion of the statistical convergence. This is an area that needs further study.

There are other social costs associated with dropouts. Higher rates of unemployment and lower earnings mean less tax revenue, loss of productivity, and increased expenditures for social welfare programs. Dropouts also have more health problems than do nondropouts. Recent projections of both economic and demographic trends suggest likely increases in these social costs. As the U.S. economy increases its reliance on highly skilled labor, for example, workers without diplomas will face greater challenges in finding work. At the same time, the populations among whom dropout rates are highest are projected to increase (Rumberger, 2000:3).

Research on the characteristics of students who drop out is suggestive of other, more subtle negative outcomes as well. Survey questions asked of students in the High-School and Beyond Study conducted by NCES, for example, reveal that dropouts have significantly lower self-esteem than do students who remain in school and are more likely than those students to believe that their fate is out of their control (Ekstrom et al., 1987:58). Such findings do not establish that dropping out causes poor self-esteem and the like; rather, they lend support to the notion that dropping out is a process and that it is the culmination of a series of misfortunes and missed opportunities on the part of students, parents, teachers, and schools.

More important, these findings show clearly why dropping out is and should be considered a problem, regardless of either uncertainty about causation or differences of opinion regarding the nature and degree of education that is appropriate for different students. There is much to be said about the apparent tension between raising academic standards for all students and allowing sufficient flexibility in the system to accommodate students with differing strengths, motivation, and goals; it is also likely that a diploma by itself is of less value for a student who has not actually mastered defined academic objectives than for one who has. Nevertheless, entering adulthood without a diploma or with a lesser alternative to one is associated with serious economic and other consequences that can be discerned throughout life.

RECOMMENDATIONS

While the consequences of dropping out of school have been well established, as have the ways in which earning a GED credential in lieu of a traditional diploma may affect later outcomes, the nature and implications of other alternatives to graduation have not. In view of the significant numbers of students who are currently availing themselves of these alternatives, it is important to understand what they involve.

Recommendation 1: The committee recommends to states and districts and to both researchers and funders of research that priority be placed on collecting key data that are disaggreggated to allow monitoring of such populations as different minority groups, English-language learners, and students with disabilities. These data should cover:

- which students and how many students are receiving credentials, including GED certification, that are significantly different from the generally prevailing standards for high school graduation;
- the nature of the academic requirements that lead to such credentials, and the extent to which those requirements are different from the generally prevailing academic standards for high school graduation;
- the processes by which students are directed to or choose to pursue such alternate credentials; and
- the later educational and employment outcomes for the students who receive these credentials.

Studies show that although GED certification can be beneficial for many students, it has less value than a standard diploma as a tool for pursuing both education and employment. It is important that policy makers, educators, parents, and students be aware of the distinctions among available credentials.

Recommendation 2: The committee recommends that officials at the school, district, and state levels disaggregate the data they already collect on school completers by the type of certificate awarded, including those awarded for passing the GED, and should make clear what knowledge and skills are represented by each credential. States, schools, and districts should also distinguish between GED holders and high school graduates in reporting data on school completion. These data should be disaggregated to allow monitoring of such populations as different minority groups, English-language learners, and students with disabilities.

3

Complexities in Counting

U nderstanding both how many students are currently dropping out and trends in dropout rates over time is critical to discussions of policies and practices and their effects. Yet this information is not as simple to obtain as one might expect. Because rates of school completion or dropping out are counted in a variety of ways, it is difficult both to compare rates for different groups or to be precise in tracking change and identifying correlations. Statistical overviews, such as the reports from the National Center for Education Statistics (NCES), provide several kinds of information and note that the results vary depending on what is measured.

COUNTING METHODS

Three rates are the most frequently used in discussions of school completion. One is the *event dropout rate,* the number of students in a particular category who were enrolled but left school without completing the requirements within a specified period of time. The second is the *status dropout rate,* which indicates the percentage of young people who are of age to be enrolled in or have completed school but are not attending and have not received a diploma. (The NCES report counts young people aged 16-24 for each year in calculating this rate.) The third is the *high school completion rate,* which indicates the proportion of students in a certain age category (such as 18 to 24) who have received a diploma or other credential (such as a GED diploma). Table 3-1 describes these and two other methods.

Although each rate is useful, the existence of these different ways of counting dropouts is a source of confusion. Press coverage of dropout

TABLE 3-1 Methods of Counting High School Dropouts

Rate	Who Is Counted	Comments
Event Dropout Rate (annual)	Students in a given grade or in a given age span who were enrolled and failed to complete the year's requirements	Difficulty of tracking whereabouts of students who leave affects count. May overcount dropouts if students who transfer to other jurisdictions or otherwise later complete school are counted. Results vary depending on which grades are included, time of year data are collected, etc.
School Completion Rate	Students who reach a particular age and have received a certificate	Typically does not distinguish by type of credential. Selection of age can result in overcount or undercount for some purposes.
Status Dropout Rate	Students who reach a particular age without having received a certificate and are not enrolled in school	Selection of age range yields differing results. Typically does not distinguish by type of certificate. Avoids difficulties caused by student transfers.
On-time Graduation Rate (longitudinal)	Students who graduate in a given year and were enrolled in ninth grade 3 years earlier	Difficulty of tracking whereabouts of students who leave affects count. Difficult to account for students not counted as ninth graders, such as those enrolled in nongraded programs, those who dropped out earlier, immigrants, etc.
Attrition Rate (longitudinal)	Students who were enrolled in an earlier grade, usually ninth, and are no longer enrolled by twelfth grade	Difficult to account for students enrolled in nongraded programs (i.e., not counted as ninth graders). Difficulty of tracking whereabouts of students who leave affects count.

statistics rarely distinguishes among the different measures or clearly accounts for discrepancies in the numbers produced by different methods. Papers and reports produced in an academic context also sometimes refer to particular dropout rates without making clear exactly who was being counted.

The rate used is important for a number of reasons. First, as discussed below, the number of students counted as dropouts can vary quite significantly depending on which measure is used. Kaufman (2000) has reported, for example, that in 1999, 85.9 percent of 18- to 24-year-olds received some sort of certificate (including alternatives such as the GED and others). If only those who received traditional diplomas are counted, however, the figure is 76.8 percent. When dropout rates are used as indicators of the relative success of reforms or other programs, the discrepant numbers can lead to vastly different conclusions. Dropout rates are also an important means of gauging the outcomes for cohorts of students; the needs of students who are incorrectly classified as school completers are likely not to be met.

SOURCES OF DATA

The principal sources of national-level data about dropping out are produced by the U.S. Census Bureau (the Current Population Survey [CPS]) and the National Center for Education Statistics (NCES) (the Common Core of Data and Longitudinal Studies Program). The CPS is an annual survey of a nationally representative sample of all U.S. households. An adult in each of 50,000 households sampled is asked for information about many things, including the schooling of household members over the age of three. This survey has been done annually for several decades, and is, Kaufman explained, "the only source of long-term trends in dropout and completion rates" (Kaufman, 2000:4).

However, Kaufman also described several complications in the CPS that need to be kept in mind. First, as with any such questionnaire, the categories chosen can have major effects on the results. The CPS, for example, asks about school enrollment for young people aged 15 to 24, so it doesn't specifically collect data about dropouts younger than 15. The survey also asks about the school completion rate for young people aged 18 to 24, but Kaufman points out that there are pros and cons to doing so. If a younger age span were selected, the survey could provide early warning about potential problems, though it might overestimate the noncompletion rate by including students who will subsequently graduate. An older age span (including people up to age 30, for example) could be chosen to avoid counting students who will eventually complete high school, but it would have other disadvantages, most notably that the outcomes for these students would reflect policies 10 or more years in the past. Most important, however, Kaufman explained, is the fact that changes in the wording of survey questions on the CPS that were made early in the 1990s have disrupted the trend line for much of the data produced by the survey.[1]

Kaufman also discusses several complications in the use of CPS data to report state-level data. First, since the CPS sampling procedures were designed for a national population, the sample sizes for some states are not large enough to yield stable results. Thus the margins of error for the state calculations are large, which means that comparisons among these results should be viewed with care. He noted, for example, that the apparently large difference between the rates for Mississippi (82 percent) and Nebraska (93 percent) are not actually statistically significant. Moreover, because the data reflect the status of 18- to 24-year-olds, they may offer limited useful information about schooling in a particular state. The young people whose status is counted may be out-of-state college students, migrant workers, or others who have not actually attended the state's public schools.

The NCES's Longitudinal Studies Program includes two studies, High School and Beyond and the National Education Longitudinal Study, that use surveys to track a variety of information about cohorts of students as they move through school. Both studies count as nondropouts students who were enrolled in "an alternative program leading to an equivalency certificate" and those who received an equivalency certificate, including a GED diploma (Kaufman, 2000). However, as noted above, looking separately at these different groups of students is important. The longitudinal data provided by these studies are nevertheless valuable, Kaufman explained, because they allow a closer look at developments such as exceptions to the recent general decline in dropout rate among low-income and low-achieving students.

---

[1]There were two principal changes. The first (1992) related to the way in which respondents indicated the level of education they had completed and resulted in a decreased (and apparently more accurate) status dropout rate. In 1994, several changes in data collection methods (use of computer-assisted telephone interviewing and adjustments for undercounts, for example) resulted in increased dropout rates which may also reflect more accurate counts (Dynarski, 2000:8-9).

NCES also sponsors a survey called the Common Core of Data, through which statistical information is collected from the departments of education in each state, the District of Columbia, and U.S. territories. NCES is also working with states to develop uniform means of collecting data on dropouts. Twenty-six states are currently participating, and Kaufman explained that when all 50 are participating, the data will allow more precise state-by-state comparisons than are currently available from the CPS data, as well as national data. Table 3-1 (above) shows the definitions of a dropout that have been developed for this data collection effort.

COMPLICATIONS

Clearly, a primary reason that counting dropouts is not straightforward is that defining them is not. If GED recipients are counted as school completers (nondropouts), for example, the resulting data will obscure the fact that part of the narrowing of the gap between black and white students' completion rates is attributable to the rise in GED certification among blacks. Since, as we have noted, GED certification has less value in the marketplace than a traditional diploma and may have other implications for life chances, this way of counting obscures an important difference. The existence of other alternatives to the traditional diploma, such as diplomas that represent a lesser degree of academic achievement, may further complicate matters. Alternative programs and certificates may play a valuable role for many students. Nevertheless, if these credentials also have less economic value than traditional diplomas, and possibly other negative implications for students' futures, the inability to distinguish the outcomes for students who receive these credentials from those for other students will be a significant impediment to understanding dropping out and school completion.

A further complication was pointed out by workshop discussant David Grissmer, who noted that the CPS does not collect data on those who join the military. He explained that since the 1960s, the policies for admission and recruitment into the military (including requirements regarding diplomas and GED certificates) have changed markedly, as has the composition of the entering population. If the effects of the military's policies, and the changing proportions of dropouts and various population subgroups in its ranks were factored in, Grissmer suggested, some national trends might look noticeably different, though this analysis has not been done.

Moreover, dropout and school completion statistics now make no distinction among the reasons that students failed to complete school or receive a diploma. Fine (1987) and many others have identified categories of students who leave school not entirely of their own volition. Such students, often called "pushouts," include students who have presented significant discipline problems, students who have been reassigned to special education programs (in some cases because they are discipline problems rather than because of a diagnosed disability), and students who are discouraged from continuing in school by formal policies or informal practices. The category of pushouts may also include students who are expelled or suspended. The relative dearth of data about these students is another piece of the puzzle observers face when they try to understand the problem of dropouts.

Recent controversies about the meaning of differing accounts of the dropout rate in the state of Texas illustrate well the nature of the problem. The state calculates an annual dropout rate for all students (for 1997-1998) of 1.6 percent (Smisko, 2000). The rate is based on reports from the districts that must explain why all students who left the district's schools did so and list the criteria by which students are classified as dropouts; see Box 3-1. Smisko also reported that, as has been widely reported elsewhere, dropout rates in Texas have declined both for the student population as a whole and for African American and Hispanic students over the past decade or so.

BOX 3-1
Criteria for Identifying Dropouts in the State of Texas

- A student who is absent without approved excuse or documented transfer and does not return to school by the following year
- A student who completes the school year but fails to reenroll the following year
- A student who leaves to enter the military before graduation
- A student from a special education, ungraded, or alternative education program who leaves school
- A student who leaves school and enters a program not qualifying as an elementary/secondary school (e.g., cosmetology school)
- A student enrolled as a migrant, whose whereabouts are unknown

SOURCE: Smisko, 2000:4.

Other observers have considered the available data about enrollment and school completion in Texas and come to quite different conclusions. For example, Haney (2001) has questioned the means by which Texas counts its dropouts, arguing that many school leavers who should be counted as dropouts are not. He has also done a number of calculations that yield a significantly more sobering picture of the rate of school completion in Texas, noting particularly that many minority students are not faring as well as the Texas reports indicate. Haney uses data on enrollment in each grade to show the rate at which white, black, and Hispanic students progress from grade to grade. He also examined the proportion of students enrolled in the ninth grade who later graduated on time for successive age cohorts by race. Using this measure, Haney found not only that the proportion of students graduating on time had declined slightly for all groups, but also that the rates for black and Hispanic students (generally about 50%) are significantly lower than those for whites (generally about 70%) (Haney, 2000).

Haney further found that a significant change in the rate at which black and Hispanic students progress from grade to grade has occurred since the mid-1980s (at which time their rates were only slightly lower than those for white students). Specifically: "By the end of the 1990s 25-30% of Black and Hispanic students, as compared with only 10% of White students, were being retained to repeat grade 9, instead of being promoted to grade 10" (Haney, 2000:5).

Haney argues that official Texas dropout calculations exclude many students. While those who reach the twelfth grade on time are graduating in greater numbers, he argues, those who are retained or leave the system earlier have become both less likely to graduate and more likely to be minorities (Haney, 2001:12-13). Haney does not attempt to account for all of the children who leave the system before grade 12 but believes that most are dropouts. The difficulties of accounting for students who leave a system mean lack of information not only about dropouts but also about students who complete their education elsewhere. Haney's work does, however, clearly demonstrate the importance of seemingly technical decisions about which students to count.

Still others have raised questions about Haney's methodology. For example, Carnoy et al. (2001) have disputed both Haney's claim that Texas's dropout rates have increased since 1990 and his claim that the Texas Assessment of Academic Skills is partly responsible. Smisko reports changes Texas is making in the way the state keeps track of school leavers designed to capture more detailed information. A recent report by the Texas Education Agency (2000) addresses many of the questions that have been raised about the data. It recommends, for example, that the state "add a Grade 9-12 Longitudinal Completion/Student Status Rate" (Texas Education Agency, 2000:2). The report recommends other improvements to data collection efforts designed to improve the state's success at keeping track of all students.

Kaufman provides another example of the difficulty in his discussion of similar disputes over dropout rates in California. Noting that differing calculations could rightly leave the public wondering whether the dropout rate was "12 percent and falling or 33 percent and rising," he pointed out some of the practical difficulties that face states, apart from the definitional ones already discussed:

> Resources are such that many schools cannot track all of their dropouts. While some schools may indeed engage in the "shell game" that their detractors accuse them of—moving dropouts to alternative programs and letting them slip away—many schools just did not know what happened to all of their "no-shows" [students who completed any of grades 7-11 but did not attend the following year] (Kaufman, 2000:31).

Kaufman's view is that no one statistical method can provide a full and accurate picture of the ways in which U.S. students move through and out of school. He believes that measures of on-time graduation, dropout, and eventual completion are all necessary, and the committee would expand his notion to include measures that provide greater detail about the different pathways students take. The larger point, however, is that it is very difficult for nonexperts to evaluate and compare rates that are calculated in different ways.

RECOMMENDATIONS

The committee concludes that current means of collecting state-, district-, and national-level data on students' progress through school and into the workforce, while valuable, are insufficient to inform policy makers and the public.

Recommendation 3: The committee recommends that policy makers, researchers, and funders of research consider the urgent need for the following kinds of additional data (disaggregated to allow monitoring of such populations as different minority groups, English-language learners, and students with disabilities):

- data that allow valid comparisons across states and, possibly, across smaller jurisdictions;
- longitudinal data that allow tracking of a greater diversity of student pathways, such as participation in alternatives to traditional secondary schooling and the earning of alternatives to the traditional diploma;
- data that allow separate reporting on the progress of students who follow such alternate pathways, both while they are in school and after they leave school, whether they are employed, unemployed, or participating in postsecondary education;
- data that allow improved tracking of students at risk for dropping out because of factors that may be apparent in elementary and middle school, such as temporary dropping out in early grades, absenteeism, retention in grade, and the like. Such data could assist jurisdictions in identifying populations of students in need of intervention and in evaluating the success of their efforts to intervene. Such data could also be used to improve public understanding of school completion and the demands on school systems.

Part of the difficulty with currently available data is that they are collected by a variety of entities for a variety of purposes at the state, district, and school levels, as well as the federal level. The adoption of a single measure that would allow comparisons across jurisdictions would address some of the difficulties in the current policy discussion, but it would have negative consequences as well. The measures exist because of the complexities of what needs to be measured, and each provides valuable information. CEETE concludes that more, not less, information about dropout behavior is needed, but believes that greater clarity and coordination is needed as well.

Recommendation 4: The committee recommends that the U.S. Department of Education provide leadership and oversight to coordinate data collection and establish long-term objectives for collecting district, state, and national data on school completion. Data available from the U.S. Department of Labor should be considered as part of this effort.

4
Effects of High-Stakes Testing and Standards

T he education reform movement has made the needs of students at risk for academic failure a key focus. Both nationally and at the state and district levels, many elements of reform have been devised with the goal of improving the performance of students who have been left behind in the past; keeping young people in school and helping all students reach high standards have been explicit goals. Standards-based reform has held out the promise of helping educators and policy makers to strengthen academic programs and to make public education more equitable than it has ever been. By making expectations for all students explicit, reforms have helped many jurisdictions understand the educational needs of the range of students they serve. Well constructed and properly used standards-based tests, by providing data about the outcomes of educational programs, can assist policy makers, administrators, and teachers in ensuring that all students are offered what they need to meet established goals and to make needed improvements in teaching, curricula, and other program elements.

However, by themselves, tests do not improve student achievement. They provide information that, together with information from other sources, can be used to improve curriculum, teaching, and learning. In some cases, however, adoption of test requirements has outpaced other reforms (*Education Week*, 2001). That is, testing is in many cases less expensive or simpler to adopt than are other reforms. Ensuring that curricula are aligned with standards and tests, ensuring that students have been taught the material and skills for which they are being held responsible, ensuring that needed resources are in place, modifying teaching strategies, and the like can all present challenges much larger than those that come with instituting new testing requirements. Meeting these challenges, however, is what will ultimately improve teaching and learning.

PURPOSES OF TESTING

Reliance on test results for a variety of purposes, including determining which students are eligible for promotion to the next grade and for graduation, has been growing in many states. Such testing can have important implications for students already experiencing academic difficulty— the students most likely to fail those tests. Understanding the effects of tests on dropout rates is complicated not only by difficulties with the available means of counting dropouts, but also by the complexity of testing itself. Tests are used for a variety of purposes, described in Box 4-1, and these purposes lead to differing consequences for students. Moreover, even

---

BOX 4-1
The Principal Purposes for Educational Tests

• *Accountability*—providing evidence of the performance of teachers, administrators, schools, districts, or states, relative to established standards or benchmarks, or in comparison to others, or both.
• *Decisions about students*—providing data that is used in making important decisions about individual students, such as placement in academic programs, grade promotion, or graduation.
• *Program evaluation*—providing evidence of the outcome of a particular educational program in terms of student performance.
• *Tracking of long-term trends*—providing evidence of changes in the performance of groups of students, such as those enrolled in a particular grade, school or school district, or those belonging to population subgroups, etc.
• *Diagnosis*—providing information about students' strengths and weaknesses with regard to specific material or skills (such as proficiency in English, for example), for use in improving teaching and learning.

SOURCE: National Research Council, 2000:20.

tests used ostensibly for the same purpose can have very different effects, depending on how they are applied, constructed, and used. Tests may be closely aligned to the skills and curriculum students are required to cover and be administered to students who have had adequate opportunity to learn the required material. They may be valid and reliable for the purposes for which they are being used, and they may successfully distinguish among students who have made a good effort to learn and those who have not. Unfortunately, in some cases these conditions are not met. Test results may penalize students who are the victims of ill-prepared teachers, poorly run schools or districts, or other circumstances beyond their control.

Professional guidelines for the use of high-stakes tests have been developed by the American Educational Research Association, the American Psychological Association, and the National Council on Measurement in Education (1999), and were outlined in the report of the National Research Council (1999). While these vital professional standards were well explicated, and may be widely known, a few key elements are worth highlighting here because the committee observes that they are not uniformly adhered to. Of particular importance in the context of a discussion of dropouts is the need for measures to:

• ensure that at every grade level early monitoring and intervention, remediation, and other supports are in place for students at risk for failing a test being used for a high-stakes purpose;

• ensure that necessary changes in teaching and curriculum have been made so that students have adequate opportunity to learn the material on which they are being tested before such tests are used in making promotion or graduation decisions;

• ensure that students for whom English is a second language or who have disabilities that affect their schooling are tested only in ways that comport with professional standards regarding inclusion and accommodations; and

• ensure that students are given sufficient opportunities to demonstrate mastery of required content and skills—that is, that a test is not used as the sole criterion for high-stakes decisions about students.

HIGH SCHOOL EXIT EXAMINATIONS

It is possible that exit or graduation tests play a role in students' decisions about dropping out. Such tests are currently growing in popularity, but the idea of using a test to determine who is eligible for a diploma is not a new one. Beginning in the 1970s, a number of states used tests of basic skills, often called minimum competency testing, as a requirement for graduation. Eighteen states now use them and 11 more are developing them (Bishop et al., 2000).[1] These tests were generally intended to ensure that graduating students had mastered the basic literacy and other skills that are considered the minimum necessary for citizenship and employment; they were not typically the sole criterion for graduation (Linn, 2000). States and districts have been making many changes to their requirements but in general seem to be moving toward more challenging exit exams. In recent years a number of states have developed new, more stringent exit examinations or have made existing tests more challenging (National Research Council 1999:164). These newer tests are intended to measure mastery of the more complex knowledge and skills that are detailed in standards documents.

The National Research Council report also addressed the question of how such tests might affect dropout rates. That report found that while a number of studies have explored the question, the results have been somewhat mixed, and further research is clearly needed. Because most of the more stringent exit exams were either recently implemented or are still in the development stages (many states have delayed the year in which students would first be required to pass the exam to graduate), most of the available research has focused on minimum competency tests. While an association between test failure and dropping out is often evident, the committee found that a clear causal connection between exit testing and dropout rates has not been conclusively established (National Research Council, 1999:174).

Bishop et al. (2000) explore the effects of policies associated with school reform, including exit exams that measure basic skills, on students' "schooling, learning, and earning." They present a wealth of data on differences in various outcomes for students who had been exposed to minimum competency exams. They find that these tests may have the effect of increasing dropout rates for some students. They also find that such tests seem to be associated with improved college attendance and increased earnings for students who pass them. They argue that, in general, such tests seem to have

---

[1]Change is rapid; 20 states are listed in a recent *Education Week* (2001) survey as requiring exit examinations.

the effect of strengthening curricula and, in other ways, improving student learning and thus the value of a high school diploma (Bishop et al., 2000). However, there are other possible explanations for these findings. One is that dropout rates may be higher in states that administer exit exams. If fewer low-achieving students are part of the population that takes such tests by the time they are administered, then the pass rates of those who remain will be higher, even if the achievement of those who actually take the test has not improved.

The workshop discussion on this point made it clear that further research is needed before firm conclusions can be reached about the effects of testing on dropout rates. The testing programs that are being implemented around the country are intended to increase learning and to prod educators to offer and students to take more demanding coursework. The desired outcome is that fewer students will drop out, both because their academic needs will be better met and because they will be motivated to work harder. However, many observers worry that students with low economic status and other risk factors will be disproportionately likely to fail exit and promotion tests and that the result will be "differential effects on grade progression and on high-school dropout" (Hauser, 2000:9). It is important to note here that group differences in test performance do not necessarily indicate problems with a test. Test scores may reflect actual differences in achievement, which could, in turn, be the result of deficiencies in or lack of access to particular coursework or instruction (National Research Council, 1999:5). Currently available data do not provide answers to many focused questions about the relationship between explicit exit examination requirements and dropout rates and do not take account of the increasing number of alternate pathways that may account for the decrease in dropout rates, particularly among black and Hispanic students.

In considering the need for additional data about school completion, it is important to note one population of students who have not traditionally been classed among dropouts: students who complete the requirements for twelfth grade but are unable to pass an examination that is a requirement for the diploma. Many states that use exit examinations—New York, Maryland, and others—have made provisions for remedial assistance, multiple opportunities for students to take the examinations, and other supports. It seems clear that the specific ways in which an exit exam is implemented are important. Nevertheless, among the students who fail will be some, perhaps many, who would otherwise have graduated. Little information is available to indicate how many such students there are, either within jurisdictions or across the nation. However, since pass rates on exit examinations (and other educational tests) are consistently lower for low-income students, minority students, English-language learners, and students with disabilities, the likelihood is that nongraduates who have completed all course requirements will be drawn disproportionately from among those same students. More detailed information about how many students are in this category in each of the states that rely on exit examinations is needed. Improved understanding of the possible differences between these students and students who drop out of school before the end of twelfth grade, and about the effects of failing the exam on these students' future education and employment, will be an important part of understanding the effects of exit exams.

Recommendation 5: The committee recommends that jurisdictions that administer exit exams collect data on students who complete the twelfth grade but fail exit exams and so do not graduate (disaggregated to allow monitoring of such populations as different minority groups, English-language learners, and students with disabilities).

RETENTION IN GRADE

There is another kind of high-stakes testing that can play an important role in students' progress. A significant body of research has addressed the relationship between retaining students in grade—that is, not promoting them to the next grade—and their subsequent educational progress. The National Research Council report (1999) found that the use of tests as requirements for grade promotion, both at the state and district levels, is increasing and explored data showing the rates at which students are retained in grade at various stages of schooling. Grade retention is pervasive in American schools, and it is more common among black and Hispanic youngsters than among whites. The report also documents the considerable evidence that students who are retained in grade (even as early as elementary school) perform less well in school (even when results are controlled for age and number of grades completed) and are significantly more likely to drop out of school.

According to a variety of census and other data that Hauser (1999) has assembled, there was a substantial increase between 1972 and 1996 in the numbers and percentages of students who were at least one grade behind most other children their age. Moreover, there are significant differences, by race and gender, in the rates at which students fall behind. These differences appear in the early primary grades and increase as students move through school. Among 15- to 17-year-olds, about 50 percent of black males and 30 percent of white females are at least one grade behind most students their age. Hauser further shows that students who are retained in any grade are significantly more likely to drop out of school than those who are not, even when factors such as sex, race and ethnicity, social background, cognitive ability, and other factors are controlled.[2]

Valencia (2000) also argues that retaining students in grade is a very strong predictor of the subsequent choice to drop out of school. He notes further that African American and Mexican American children in Texas are significantly more likely to be retained in grade than are white children. Valencia's concern, based on his findings, is that as Texas and other states place increasing reliance on standardized tests in making their decisions about whether to retain students or promote them to the next grade, the result will be an increase in retention, a corresponding increase in the dropout rate as the students affected move through the system, and a disparate effect on subgroups of the population that are already vulnerable (Valencia, 2000). Other scholars have reinforced the connection between retention in grade at any level and the subsequent decision to drop out (Rumberger, 2000, 2001). Although the precise relationship between graduation testing and dropping out of school is still in dispute, there is no dispute that retention in grade is a very strong predictor of who will drop out.

Conclusion: Given the difficulty and cost of preventing students from dropping out once the process of disengagement from school has begun, it is clear that neither requiring a student to retake the grade nor promoting a failing student is, by itself, a sufficient response to his or her academic difficulty. The value and importance of addressing struggling students' difficulties directly and specifically as soon as they are apparent are paramount. Moreover, the strong association between retention in grade and dropping out suggests that retention is usually not a beneficial intervention.

---

[2]Hauser cites one study (Temple et al., 1998) that finds an increase of 12 percentage points and another (Anderson, 1994) that finds a 70 percent increase in likeliness to drop out for students who repeat a grade.

SUMMING UP

Distinctions among different kinds of tests are key to understanding the effects they may have on students. The effects of more rigorous, content-based tests may be very different from the effects of basic skills tests. The way in which testing programs are aligned with curricular requirements and standards, as well as other aspects of the educational system, are also central for understanding their effects. To be truly informative, evaluations of the effects of exit tests should clearly distinguish among tests of different kinds, used for different purposes, and should draw on data about each category of students who might be affected by such tests.

At this early stage in the progress of many state reforms, there is insufficient evidence to determine what effect, if any, exit examinations have on dropout rates. Indeed, the likelihood is that the effects of these tests will vary significantly, depending on the ways in which they are constructed and implemented and on the ways in which their results are used. However, there is reason to believe that both exit testing and other high-stakes testing may sometimes be used in ways that have unintended harmful effects on students at risk for academic failure because of poverty, lack of proficiency in English, disability, and membership in population subgroups that have been educationally disadvantaged.

Changes in dropout rates, or in the characteristics of the students who drop out, may be signs both of the effects—positive or negative, intended or not—of new standards or exit exams and of how well schools are helping students to meet higher standards. Any such changes should be carefully monitored and evaluated as jurisdictions progress with their reforms. However, inferences of cause and effect should be made with care. The progress of students' schooling and the influences that lead some of them to drop out are complex. Moreover, the available statistics that can reveal changes in dropout patterns are likewise complex and should be interpreted carefully. The committee hopes that the recommendations in this report will be a useful tool for those who seek to improve understanding of school completion.

References

American Council on Education
    2001   <http://www.acenet.edu/calec/ged.intro-A.html>. [Accessed 11/29/2000.]
American Educational Research Association, American Psychological Association, and National Council on Measurement in Education
    1999   *Standards for Educational and Psychological Testing.* Washington, DC: American Psychological Association.
Anderson, D. K.
    1994   Paths Through Secondary Education: Race/Ethnic and Gender Differences. Unpublished doctoral thesis, University of Wisconsin, Madison.
Balfanz, R., and N. Legters
    2001   How Many Central City High Schools Have a Severe Dropout Problem, Where Are They Located, and Who Attends Them? Initial Estimates Using the Common Core of Data. Paper prepared for the forum of The Civil Rights Project of Harvard University and Achieve, Inc., entitled Dropouts in America: How Severe is the Problem? What Do We Know About Intervention and Prevention? Cambridge, MA (January 13).
Bishop, J., F. Mane, and M. Bishop
    2000   Stakes for Students: Impacts on Schooling, Learning and Earning. Paper presented at the School Completion in Standards-Based Reform: Facts and Strategies Workshop, National Research Council, Washington, DC (July 17). Available: Cornell University.
Cameron, S., and J. Heckman
    1993   The nonequivalence of high school equivalents. *Journal of Labor Economics* 11(1):1-47.

Carnoy, M., S. Loeb, and T. Smith
    2001   Do Higher Test Scores in Texas Make for Better High School Outcomes? Paper prepared for the forum of The Civil Rights Project of Harvard University and Achieve, Inc. entitled Dropouts in America: How Severe is the Problem? What Do We Know About Intervention and Prevention? Harvard University, Cambridge, MA (January 13).

Chaplin, D.
    1999   GEDs for Teenagers: Are There Unintended Consequences? Paper presented at the annual meeting of the Association for Public Policy Analysis and Management, Washington, DC (November). Available at <http://www.urban.org/education/ged.html>. [Accessed 7/26/2000.]

Dorn, S.
    2000   Historical Perspectives on School Completion in Standards-Based Reform. Paper presented at the School Completion in Standards-Based Reform: Facts and Strategies Workshop, National Research Council, Washington, DC (July 17). Available: University of South Florida.

Dynarski, M.
    2000   How Can We Help? What We Have Learned from Federal Dropout-Prevention Programs. Paper presented at the School Completion in Standards-Based Reform: Facts and Strategies Workshop, National Research Council, Washington, DC (July 17). Available: Mathematica Policy Research.

Education Week
    2000   Lessons of a Century: A Nation's Schools Come of Age. Bethesda, MD: Editorial Projects in Education.
    2001   Quality Counts 2001: A Better Balance. Editorial Projects in Education, Vol. XX (17), January 11, 2001.

Ekstrom, R., M. Goertz, J. Pollack, and D. Rock
    1987   Who drops out of high school and why? Findings from a national study. In *School Dropouts: Patterns and Policies*, G. Natriello, ed. New York: Teachers College Press, Columbia University.

ERIC Digest
    1987   The Dropout's Perspective on Leaving School. Highlights: An ERIC/CAPS Digest. ED 291015. Available: <http://www.ed.gov/databases/ERIC_Digests/ed291015.html>. [Accessed 1/3/2001.]

Fine, M.
    1987   Why urban adolescents drop into and out of public high school. In *School Dropouts: Patterns and Policies*, G. Natriello, ed. New York: Teachers College Press, Columbia University.

Haney, W.
    2000   The myth of the Texas miracle in education. *Education Policy Analysis Archives* 8(41): August 19.
    2001   Revisiting the Myth of the Texas Miracle in Education: Lessons About Dropout Research and Dropout Prevention. Paper prepared for the forum of The Civil Rights Project of Harvard University and Achieve, Inc., entitled Dropouts in America: How Severe is the Problem? What Do We Know About Intervention and Prevention? Harvard University, Cambridge, MA (January 13).

Hauser, R.
    1999   Should We End Social Promotion? Truth and Consequences. Center for Demography and Ecology Working Paper No. 99-6, University of Wisconsin-Madison (October).
    2000   On Calculating High School Dropout and Completion Rates. Paper presented at the School Completion in Standards-Based Reform: Facts and Strategies Workshop, National Research Council, Washington, DC (July 17). Available: Department of Sociology, University of Wisconsin.

Kaufman, P.
    2000   Calculating High School Dropout and Completion Rates: The Complexities of Data and Definitions. Paper presented at the School Completion in Standards-Based Reform: Facts and Strategies Workshop, National Research Council, Washington, DC (July 17). Available: MPR Associates.

Lee, V. E., and D. T. Burkam
    2001   Dropping Out of High School: The Role of Organization and Structure. Paper prepared for the forum of The Civil Rights Project of Harvard University and Achieve, Inc., entitled Dropouts in America: How Severe is the Problem? What Do We Know About Intervention and Prevention? Harvard University, Cambridge, MA (January 13).

Linn, R. L.
    2000   Assessment and accountability. *Educational Researcher* 29 (2):4-16.

McPartland, J., and W. Jordan
    2001   Essential Components of High School Dropout Prevention Reforms. Paper prepared for the forum of The Civil Rights Project of Harvard University and Achieve, Inc., entitled Dropouts in America: How Severe is the Problem? What Do We Know About Intervention and Prevention? Harvard University, Cambridge, MA (January 13).

Murnane, R., J. Willett, and K. Boudett
    1995   Do high school dropouts benefit from obtaining a GED? *Educational Evaluation and Policy Analysis* 17(2) (Summer):133-147.

Murnane, R., J. Willett, and J. Tyler
    1999   Who Benefits From Obtaining a GED? Evidence From High School and Beyond. Working Paper 7172. National Bureau of Economic Research, Cambridge, MA.

National Center for Education Statistics
    1996   *A Comparison of High School Dropout Rates in 1982 and 1992.* NCES 96-893. Washington, DC: U.S. Department of Education.
    2000   *Dropout Rates in the United States: 1999.* NCES 2001-022. Washington, DC: U.S. Department of Education.

National Research Council
    1999   *High Stakes: Testing for Tracking, Promotion, and Graduation.* Committee on Appropriate Test Use, Jay P. Heubert and Robert M. Hauser, eds., Board on Testing and Assessment, National Research Council. Washington, DC: National Academy Press.
    2000   *Testing English-Language Learners in U.S. Schools: Report and Workshop Summary.* Committee on Educational Excellence and Testing Equity. Kenji Hakuta and

Alexandra Beatty, eds., Board on Testing and Assessment, Center for Education. Washington, DC: National Academy Press.

Pettit, B., and B. Western

2001 Inequality in Lifetime Risks of Incarceration. Paper presented at meeting of the Population Association of America, Washington, DC.

Rumberger, R.

2000 Who Drops Out of School and Why. Paper presented at the School Completion in Standards-Based Reform: Facts and Strategies Workshop, National Research Council, Washington, DC (July 17). Available: University of California, Santa Barbara.

2001 Why Students Drop Out of School and What Can Be Done. Paper prepared for the forum of The Civil Rights Project of Harvard University and Achieve, Inc., entitled Dropouts in America: How Severe is the Problem? What Do We Know About Intervention and Prevention? Harvard University, Cambridge, MA (January 13).

Smisko, Anne

2000 A Look at Reforms and Statistics in Texas. Materials presented at the School Completion in Standards-Based Reform: Facts and Strategies Workshop, National Research Council, Washington, DC (July 17). Available: Texas Education Agency, San Antonio.

Temple, J. A., A. J. Reynolds, and W. T. Miedel

1998 Can early intervention prevent high school dropout? Evidence from the Chicago child-parent centers. Institute for Research on Poverty, University of Wisconsin, Madison, Discussion paper 1180-98. November.

Texas Education Agency

2000 *Dropout Study: A Report to the 77th Texas Legislature.* San Antonio: Texas Education Agency.

Valencia, R.

2000 Legislated School Reform Via High-Stakes Testing: The Case of Pending Anti-Social Promotion Legislation in Texas and its Likely Adverse Impact on Racial/Ethnic Minority Students. Paper presented at the School Completion in Standards-Based Reform: Facts and Strategies Workshop, National Research Council, Washington, DC (July 17). Available: University of Texas.

Appendix

Workshop Agenda

School Completion in Standards-Based Reform:
Facts and Strategies
July 17-18, 2000
Washington, DC

Monday, July 17

8:00   *Continental breakfast*

8:30   *Welcome and Overview of Workshop Goals*

> Ulric Neisser, Cornell University
> William Trent, University of Illinois, Urbana-Champaign
> (Committee Cochairs)

8:45   *Historical Perspective*

> Brief review of trends in graduation during the century and public policy history of dropping out as a visible concern for policymakers and practitioners.
> Sherman Dorn, University of South Florida
> Respondent: Jay Heubert, Teachers College, Columbia University

> Questions and Discussion

10:00   *Difficulties in Calculating Dropout Rates*

Various ways of calculating the rates can yield results that appear different, even contradictory. Both clarification of current data and guidance in understanding these complexities for the interested nonstatistician are needed.

• What data are collected and how are they presented?
• What are the proper interpretations of dropout rates as currently reported in different jurisdictions?
• Why are differing data reported for the same cohorts and locales?
• What are the most accurate and useful representations of dropout statistics?

Phillip Kaufman, Director, Statistical Analysis and Data Design, MPR Associates
Respondent: Robert Hauser, University of Wisconsin, Madison

Questions and Discussion

11:00   *Break*

11:15   *Who is Dropping Out and Why?*

Which factors seem to account for the greatest variation, and what is known about how these factors influence the decision to drop out? A look at variations by cultural background and ethnicity and other factors.

Russell Rumberger, University of California, Santa Barbara
Respondent: Herbert Walberg, University of Illinois

Questions and Discussion

12:30   *Lunch*

1:00   *One State's Experience: Texas*

       A Look at Reforms and Statistics in Texas

          Anne Smisko, Texas Education Agency
          Respondent: Diana Lam, Providence School Department

       Legislated School Reform Via High-Stakes Testing: The Case
       of Pending Anti-Social Promotion Legislation in Texas and Its
       Likely Adverse Impact on Racial/Ethnic Minority Students

          Richard Valencia, University of Texas
          Respondent: William Trent

2:15   *Stakes for Students: Impacts on Schooling, Learning, and
       Earning*

       A look at the effects of acquisition of a high-school diploma
       or GED certification on future schooling, employment
       opportunities, and earning power.

          Ferran Mañe, Rovira I Virgili University
          Respondent: Henry Levin, Teachers College,
             Columbia University

          Questions and Discussion

3:30   *Break*

3:45   *Tracking Students' Progress Through School*

       What kinds of indicators of students' progress through school
       might be tracked as a way of monitoring the effects of high-
       stakes tests on school completion? A look at value-added
       measures as a means of identifying schools and students that
       are struggling.

Robert Meyer, University of Chicago
Respondent: Ulric Neisser

Questions and Discussion

5:00   *Adjourn*

Tuesday, July 18

8:30   *What's Being Done to Prevent Students From Dropping Out?*

A look at examples of successful efforts to target the needs of
students at high risk for dropping out.

Mark Dynarski, Mathematica Policy Research
Respondent: Judith Johnson, Department of Education

9:30   *Discussion of Preliminary Questions*

Discussants' responses to questions and workshop
presentations

David Grissmer, RAND
Robert Hauser, University of Wisconsin, Madison
Aaron Pallas, Michigan State University

10:30   *Break*

10:45   *General Discussion*

Moderators: Ulric Neisser, William Trent

11:45   *Concluding Remarks*

12:00   *Adjourn*